Cold Water

COLD WATER

BY Lou Lipsitz

WESLEYAN UNIVERSITY PRESS

Middletown, Connecticut

Library of Congress Catalog Card Number : 67–15228

Manufactured in the United States of America

FIRST EDITION

For Joan

Contents

Cold Water

Cold Water

Cold water on my bare feet.
You are like cold water.

All day I've watched the water
run from the tap, splash into the bushes
where the earth awaits it
and sucks it up.

Cold water! The grass exclaims.

To a Fighter Killed in the Ring

In a gym in Spanish Harlem
boys with the eyes of starved leopards
flick jabs at your ghost
chained to a sandbag.

They smell in the air the brief truth of poverty
just as you once did:
                    "The weak don't get rich."

✤

You made good.
Probably you were a bastard,
dreaming of running men down in a Cadillac
and tearing blouses off women.

And maybe in your dreams great black teeth
ran after you down dead-end alleyways
and the walls of your room
seemed about to collapse,
bringing with them a sky of garbage
and your father's leather strap.
And you sat up afraid you were dying
just as you had so many nights as a child.

✤

Small bruises to the brain.
An accumulation
of years of being hit.

I will not forget that picture of you
hanging over the ropes, eyes closed,
completely wiped out.
Like a voice
lost in the racket of a subway train
roaring on under the tenements of Harlem.

The Pipes

You will not be like those who turn their faces away
when death moves toward them like an ocean.

You will know him. You will look at him,
slowly, opening your mind little by little,
just as you sat, as a child, with the water rolling
around your legs; staring until the ocean became known to you.
And you will go back often, carrying away with you
the strange moisture of that sea
and a desire to be luminous and unarmed.

I think of the Indians of the Colombian jungle,
and their pipes of gay colors.
They will dig clay for the pipes
in one spot only,
on the territory of their enemies—
a valley guarded by traps and poisoned arrows.
They say only those pipes are real.

Skinny Poem

Skinny
poem,
all
your
ribs
showing
even
without
a
deep
breath

thin
legs
rotted
with
disease.

Live
here!
on
this
page,
barely
making
it,
like
the
mass
of
mankind.

Drunk, Two Afternoons

Drunk, two afternoons.
I am a tree gone mad because my tangled roots
have finally touched sweet water.

In the evening along the path from her house
I am blind with joy.
Her eyes sail in my veins like small, black fish
in a narrow stream.

O I will stay here forever
Growing higher
with snow in my hair.

Night Train

A flash of cobalt over the railroad crossing—
it gleams like a well-kept pistol
beside the delicate ear of a sleeping town.

The hard earth shakes and crumbles
as under the feet of a long army.
In his bed, a man sits up frightened,
sure he has heard something.

Probably the locomotive whistle—
or maybe this is the arrival
of that deep, intricate destruction
of which we all claim innocence.

Reading a Poem by Walt Whitman I Discover We Are Surrounded by Companions

Reading Walt Whitman, I find he compares his soul to a spider.
Fantastic!
Who could know he would?

And suddenly, my life tips over! a bed in a rat-infested
apartment with scared kids jumping on one end.

My head can take it—
like a cheap flowerpot with hyacinths,
uncracked after a four-story drop
from the window sill.

My heart, that was just a heart,
begins to fit everywhere, like newspapers
stuffed into the broken ceilings of Harlem.

Thinking of South Vietnam: its Dictatorship, its Oppression of the Population, the Buddhist Suicides, the Ruthlessness of the War, and Our Claim to Be Defending "Freedom" There

Why sadists Why executives of rotted nightmares Why
statues with eyes that never close Why the sick and ambitious
to stand at the head of nations?

There are dead soldiers There are strategies
with fancy names like "Operation Sunrise" that mean the same
damn thing There are magazines with color pictures
showing war can be beautiful There are bayonets growing
among men like spinal columns.

Americans, what can we say to those whose torsos have smouldered
in protest What can we say when freedom has the shape of
the escaping bullet and nourishment the form of the gnawed heart?

Pancho Villa

"I am Pancho Villa," says the truck
in crude yellow letters painted on its grill
and battles through the traffic armed
with these words—idiotic, gleeful.

Caught, it pivots proud as a dancer
in the storm of cars and buses,
then thrusts on, forcing the autos aside,
boasting, threatening, ignoring the torrents of abuse,

saying "I am Pancho Villa
the Mexican bandit, the mustachioed one.
Who would contain me? Who would know my measure?
I sweep the valleys like the coming of rain."

So, poor truck, green truck—
one drop in the metropolitan flow.
So, working heart.
So, old truculence—our thundercloud, our rainbow.

Prospect Beach

Here I slept with my face turned
        toward the sun,
my eyes closed and my arms lying
        beside me
like two different animals that
        enjoyed my smell.

What roar, ocean! What an alien
        you are.
You are clear and indecipherable
        and full of fish:
strange and fast ones; and full
        of wild plants.

I watched the striped killies
        swim near shore
and the children splashing about
        holding glass jars;
trying to catch a fish
        in a bare hand.

And I was old, with the taste of sleep
        in my mouth.
Old and solitary, shivering
        in the breeze.
There are none like me here, only
        companions and marvels.

Return

No moon.
My boots crunch on the iced-over path.
The woods are still.
I have nowhere to go.

Then from a dark place
you jump out and throw yourself on my shoulders.
You've come back.

I will carry you,
strange rider.

I

On long trains, commuters
lose consciousness.
   They dream of a satchel
   stumbled on in a cab—
   something glitters on the bottom—
   pull it open
   reach in!
                  only a lost gentleness

II

At dusk
a man who has waited a long time,
walks under the highway bridge
near water.
He moves a stick among the reeds
and leans over to look.

Not a fish.
The polluted water stares up at him,
flashing its oily smile,
like a face in a loan company ad.

O the Rahway River, like our lives,
shallow, muddy and full of shit.

III

In this bar
three guys watch TV wrestling.
Outside, in the narrow darkness,
five kids smoke cigarettes.
Across the street

one big bulb
has gone out in the neon sign
over a store.
A part of everything
is unemployed.

IV

Now it is late.
The ferry to Brooklyn crosses
the deep, oily water of the bay
moving straight toward its dock.
Lamps are switched off.
It is now that the heart may venture out,
trying to find its way—
like a man slightly drunk
who suddenly recalls
something urgent he'd forgotten
and runs into the street—
to be blinded by headlights
and cursed for blocking traffic.

A Note

Look! in the bowl on your dresser I've put
                daffodils
        and clover

                        They will be my eyes
to watch over you in the difficult night.

And I am taking with me a blackness from your hair.
I want to feel its warmth
when I ride the roads among worn and nervous men.

For B., with the Blues

You ever been down you know how I feel
—feel like an engine ain't got no drivin' wheel.
—BROWNIE MCGHEE

When I hear George Lewis blowing
his clarinet
when I listen to Kid Shots, Slow Drag
and the others beating it out—
when I listen to this old jazz
I think it's not too late! Still
there is something to grab onto—
the small, purple flowers
still make it to the surface.

The wild and gentle survive
somewhat.
Things still open—
turn outward—
doors, hands, eyes,
the light
of human bodies.

Strange joy!
In the harsh dark,
the cock can crow, sweetly,
between legs.

I Am Thinking of Chicago and of What Survives

In the shadows of old buildings, human bodies are opened
and fingered perfunctorily, like prayer books.

Near the mills, there are cash registers shining in the dimness
of bars, stolid as the helmets of soldiers at a crucifixion.

Along the railroad tracks I see poor men's windows
opening into a vacant eternity like the dusty mouths of the dead.

Yet, hidden in alleys the children practice their strange devotions
before the small churches of garbage and snow.

After Visiting a Home for Disturbed Children

Broken lamps!
Their faces shine with a destroyed light:
Illumination
of tangled gestures, of silent beatings,
of the black river of childhood.
Terrible light.

A light to which I cannot speak.
Light of corroding marriages.
Light of secret cries lost
like the signals of minute stars.
Light of empty basements
in which children have carefully hidden their names.

At night, unable to sleep,
I stare out the window at the empty road
and bits of light shine out of the dark,
intense, searching,
like the eyes of a girl who is buried alive.

Sean O'Casey

Now Sean O'Casey
    is dead whose plays and stories go on

        proclaiming themselves

dragging us
together.

        Organizers of
        open rebellion
        turning up in slums
        of the chest

        calling us

        from cramped quarters to see:
                the suffering

        see ourselves
           kneel
        before sadistic institutions, hands
        roped behind our backs, the whips
        of history shredding our skins
        for crimes we cannot understand.

O'Casey! O'Casey!

  it is true there are hearts so
  dwarfed they would fit
  in a
  billfold behind a desk in a pew or a single nation.

But remind us now of
the body's grace the joys
of manhood,
that we might cease
to hate our neighbors as ourselves.

The Young Boy

Complete, his time come, he stood up
and felt how alien he'd grown.
The daylight broke into his secret room
like police detectives,
and he stepped back
fearing the loss of what he'd been.

What could he say now with this voice
that mingled speech and obscenities
deep in his neck? the blood beating
like rioting convicts against the
penitentiary walls of his life.

He wished to be free. To speak
to walk to see to breathe to be whole.
But memories dragged him down like
stolen ingots sewn into the lining of his coat.
What times he'd had! What seas what
narrow escapes! Whipping all the prisoners
on the decisive rack of his dreams.

Now there were buses. Tools in the hand
as real as genitals.
The morning light
returning without fail to haunt him
like a well-behaved cousin
held up as an example.

Ah Pinocchio, becoming human!
Waking from dark boyhood,
fantastic confinement,
solitude of wild power,
to this wished-for, jubilant, desperate, ordinary,
shared . . . .

Young Woman on Her Own

The color worn off. You look around:

Bare trees. The beach deserted.
Summer houses abandoned in this weather.

You've stayed on alone, sick of everybody.
At the dock you smile, sitting in the small boat
that floats despite the cold waves.

Already Late

Already late, we pull up to the house.
Shadows of the night stand in the doorway,
like Indians guarding the ritual place
of the spirits.
I pick up the child.

She is sleeping
and her body is like water.
She breathes very quietly.
She is like a brook that no one
has ever seen.

As I walk
the spirits come near,
stroking her hair and singing.
They plant four young trees
beside her shore, and in the air
they place two dragonflies
with scarlet wings
to be her companions.

An hour later when the TV goes on,
I begin to weep.

The Tree Is Father to the Man

By all the laws
we should have been cracked into splinters;
broken down
into hard-working people
heads stuck
in the checkbook.

By all the laws
we should have been dead
                    (where it counts)
far down
where things grow.

O, all the laws!
But the tree showed us
                    possibilities!
Black tree
bombarbed by incinerators
standing in shadow
on a 2 x 2 plot.
Once a year
not only leaves! but fruit!
small green
apples, perfect for window cracking.

A Way of Judging Politics

The relation of man to woman is the most natural relation of human being to human being.—KARL MARX

I

As usual, Election Day
                approaches us
like a guerilla
war

We are all soldiers:

                                    the unnatural candidates
                                                    (hidden)

                                            perfect camouflage
                                                    of their
                                                                    voices;

                                by the

bewildered
citizens disarmed   in the
                        heavy
            jung-   le   o
                            f   techniqu
                                                    e
                                s.

☙

As usual
the

W-E-L-L-D-I-S-C-I-P-L-I-N-E-D-T-R-O-O-P-S
BLOCKOFF

t   s
t   t
h   r
    e
    e
    t
e   s

The State trembles like a
poisoned child
vomiting black histories

the tanks
roll
toward
the rebels
who

shield themselves

behind
an
over-
turned
bus.

II

Yet I have known the small, bright wars of love
fought by gentle soldiers
who lay naked in each other's sight despite all the risks.

Within me all the forces move toward you;
the cities of rubble forgotten,
the skin washed clear of the ferment and dust of barricades,
holding in their hands that solemn declaration the joyous body makes.

Why I Left My Job in a Garment Factory

Wings!

Mouth!

Eyes!

Cock!

Where are you?
                    Is *this* the best we can do? this dust,
this dark factory I hate,
the soaped-up windows,
100,000 skirts hanging
on iron bars over my head?

Lunch hour when we collapse,
or play cards and curse management?

Monotony and sad visions of
plaid skirts turning into teenage girls naked
from the waist up?

Aren't we poets? Haven't we demanded
"to each according to his need?"
I need to take off my shoes and love.

Winter Twilight

Over the dark highway,
over the woods
and the clusters of small houses,
the clouds appear

The great clouds of a winter twilight!

> When I see them I feel like a hundred men
> who know they have slipped out of prison
> without a trace

The great clouds—

> ragged and ancient
> like the heart,
> like the heads of old, pious men
> we cannot help loving

And everything that was forgotten takes
hold of me
I walk out into the small congregation
of the twilight
and find I must sing and weep and
speak to the dead

Our words are no steadier than our journeys
than the marriage collapsing
like a drunk over the wheel at 90 mph.

Our poems, full of halts, emergencies, far-off lights,
indecipherable smells, blind alleys,
I cannot apologize for them.
They are no worse than the thick traffic jam of losses
we are stuck in.

Our poems, shining and deadly, dense with emptiness
represent the dark interior
—the hearts of multitudes like factories at night
full of silent, black machinery and the smell of oil.

But our poems also rave at dusk, burn secretly in fields,
mad, nativistic, like hope's Ku Klux Klan
obsessed with reconstruction.

Elizabeth, N.J.

The structural and historical features of modern society must be connected with the most intimate features of man's self.

—H. GERTH and C. WRIGHT MILLS

Night.
Things break.

In refineries, crude oil is decomposed by great fires
that snap its chemical bonds.

A man wakes from the merciless heat of his dreams
with a splitting headache.

Warmed Through and Through by a Bowl of Fish Soup

If only!
      the materials for a poem were like soup!

and I could press them into a ball
without losing a drop
through my fingers.

Then I'd hit you in the kisser Splat!

      And you'd know!
      what was missing all along:
      chowder for the spirit.

Bedtime Story

Nighttime. The faithful prison guard,
Poverty, locks the Negroes in their neighborhoods.
And many white men seal themselves
in the condemned buildings of the soul.

America sleeps, the raw wounds still open.
Mississippi sheriffs enter and stalk
in the forests of dreams; Southern judges,
pounding their gavels, crush small eyes in the brain.

On a highway, a good man is overtaken
by a carload of hoodlums.
Turn away quick!
or you'll see him get it.

Goodnight.

Wild Day

I try impossible things
like racing up stairs
six at a time.

The clarinet in my body
plays the same
beautiful note all day.

You have been faithful to me
so damned long!

City Summer

Things come out.

After lunch, a young guy
in an undershirt
pisses into a pile of worn tires,
whistling.

Above the clinging adolescents
in the dark street,
an old lady watches from her window,
like a deposed princess
despising the revolution.

Under the trees
I fall on Joan by surprise,
like a caterpillar.

Political Poem

Once crime was as solitary as a cry of protest; now it is as universal as science.
—ALBERT CAMUS

Behind me I hear the sad commands
of confused military.
From a window over my head
come the edicts of the legislature of madness,
no longer able to keep itself secret.

I am running down an alley of filthy centuries;
of lies implacable as gravity.
I hear ordinary people,
turned into executioners,
rejoicing in their victories.
I see a man's hand rusting like a mineral
in the pathetic formations of politics.
I watch typhoons of whips and bewilderment
growing in the brains of children.

Behind every dream stands a battalion of deranged bones.

And I know that none of us
will ever enter the warm mouth of the sea.
We will never learn of delicate animals,
of tenderness,
of the silver children of felicities.
We will never enter
the great structure of clear eyes
that lives in the cells of our hands.

Tonight, as always, men sleep,
but nations are awake.
Loneliness drifts across the landscape
like gas.
Plans are made
and many are dying.
Like a shell fragment,
sorrow rips open the brain.
And my eyes,
two soldiers seeking shelter,
continue their journey
through the time of detonations and losses.

Not Reaching a Lake

I fall over a rock. My left foot that was healing
is twisted again.

> Lake, that I hoped to reach this morning, I cannot
> make it.
> I am lame
> and will have to do without you.

I rest on the forest floor.
Sun edges carefully into the woods. A perfect hour.
Birds burst into the air, calling. A cardinal perches near me
and I lie still, watching him preening and looking for insects.
He is undisturbed.

Elsewhere, the lame world drags itself on.

No one disturbed the world today.
Sleeping late,
dozing in afternoon chairs holding
newspapers close,
we were like small animals
hiding under stones in the rain.

And everything discolored a little.
The piece of fruit in a corner
began to grow rotten.

Night covers up our weariness.
Covers the old peach trees in backyards
that still stand, but never blossom.

And yet, far off,
the waves pound in us.
The forgotten tide comes
with its torn offerings;
and somehow we are like the sea
—silver, unknown life
flickering far down.

A Task

Potatoes. I will hunt potatoes
in the fashion of my grandmother
who fed us all.

Potatoes. Like the tough hearts of young men.
The firm core of joy in sexual love.
The world that trembles and changes.

In the fashion of my grandmother
I will abandon all exotic things

and hunt a language
of odd, true shapes that were nurtured in the old earth.

A Road

Dead ones, there is a road
without tree
without cornfield
        a dry road
        of small stones
a bare road

I will walk to you
as a blind man crossing the continent
carrying only his wits.

Dead ones, there is your ocean
on a bare road.

It is time I stood there:
a blind man
facing the sad noise of the waves.

without tree
without cornfield.

Los Angeles Riots—August, 1965

This is no special concern of mine. All it proves is what I've known for a long time. The Negroes hate me and I hate the Negroes.

         —Young suburban lawyer leaving for the beach

The cry: "GET WHITEY"

    All night thousands of Negroes burning—
    their hearts napalmed by years of scorn.
    They think it is their turn.

Now at dawn when races sleep
when nobody is awake enough to know what justice is
and people must scratch themselves to uncover who they are—
my pale skin weeps black tears
              filled with the burnt-out lives of America.

History returns. The slave ship
in revolt. Mid-voyage.
Locks are broken.
From the crowded hold fires
spread upward. Decks give way.
Men fall through into one another's
arms. Hatred takes off
his rags showing
the incinerated torso of despair.
Everything vanishes
between continents.

                But today on the white beaches
                of the New World
                a man, putting a shell
                to his ear, will be startled

by a muffled, pulsing sound,
as if blood had penetrated
a new area of his brain,
or chains were being dragged
on the ocean bottom.

For a Teacher of Disturbed Children

With the slashed eyes of their imprisonment
they tear off your toes.
But you never move,
as if there were roots in the soles of your feet.

Their impassable memories, like washed-out bridges,
overwhelm your air with brown water.
Their rigid faces, stolen from murderers waiting to die,
turn your movement into stones.

You stand stripped and tall:
a tree whose limbs have been broken by armless boys.

But you grow again:
send out new leaves and branches.
You wrap their pained eyes and their sores in your color.

You see the mind emerge from its agony,
slowly, like a sapling from the shackles of a rocky earth.
Then in place of crimes there is a world.

The Darkness of an Old Love

What a lousy tree love is!
that can never be pulled out.

The wood made of soft night
and the lonely farms
that passed into my blood
on the road to her house.

Both of us,
roots, blind,
digging into the earth.

The wood
drinking
the odor of joy.

What a lousy tree
that leaves its shadow
but no fragrance.

Fantasy for Those Who Hate Their Work

In the beginning will be the hand
of the tailor—
                    gently,
very gently,
embracing the calf of a young lady.

Then shoe salesmen
will refuse to kneel.

Clerks will
vomit tables
of multiplication
ruining their
shines.

In the middle of America
assembly lines will be covered
by the Atlantic Ocean
of laughter.

The sealed gates of the mind
WILL BE SMASHED
by waiters with serving trays.
The old banner:
                    "I work therefore I'm weary"
will be minced. . . .

Then we will speak.
Then we will raise new flags.
Then we will learn.

And I will direct revolutionary
education,
teaching the politics of limbs,
the economics of valleys,
the psychology of the sea—
and the great disciplines of friendship and drunkenness.

The Feeding

We sit in the darkness
and the baby drinks from you.
Alive! I cannot
believe it.

We are silent.
Far off, great explosives
stand in hundreds of holes
sucked out of the planet;
millions of men
who might have befriended each other
prowl the earth's surface
as hunters.

You open your eyes
and look at me
and I see you are satisfied.
The baby sleeps.
You have nourished what you can,
which is no small triumph
in a starved time.

To My Sister

You walk through the world
and see the open wounds.
You walk slowly,
looking around you.
Things seem to you
like the body of a slaughtered duck
hanging on a hook through its neck
in the window of the poultry store.

You see the many wounds hastily stitched up
with sutures of decaying love.
You walk through New York and find
mouths gaping, wet like fresh bruises.
A sky of thick soot presses tight
on the limbs of the city
like a tourniquet encrusted with gangrene.
You see children with skulls bitten into
and filled with coins; women whose body openings
are torn and stuffed with merchandise.

You walk, weighed down with cruelties,
drowning in the empty streets late at night;
following a path littered with deaths
and anonymous shadows.
And you are unaware that it is possible to heal,
and of the sturdy wings that are forming in your blood.

Sleep

I have a vision
of the entire world asleep.
Wonderful, undisturbed sleep—
The way I sleep on a winter morning.

I see millions of poor men
whose hearts are tired,
lying quietly
close to the cool surface
of the earth.

I see the leaders of nations
in the fantastic houses of state,
mouths open on their pillows.

In the area
of delivery systems,
technicians sleep underground.
And in many places I see soldiers
in their underwear,
sleeping one-by-one
on millions of cots.

And everyone is dreaming
of his childhood;
dreaming of a darkness
he cannot understand;
dreaming of old games and faces he had forgotten.

And no one stirs.
And no one is
under orders.

Poem in New York

Walker of streets,
have you entered them?
Are you the eyes
of chimneys or a broken lamp;
the mouth
of deserted shoes?

Does the city
create your face?
Does the oil of burning children
smear your forehead?
Is there in your cheek
the breath of a bird destroyed by loneliness?

And when you see the black river
in the blood of men,
are you a disaster of the stars?

Thaw in the City

Now my legs begin to walk.
The filthy piles of snow are melting.
Pavements are wet.

What clear, tiny streams!
Suddenly I feel the blood flowing in the veins
in the backs of my hands.

And I hear a voice—a wonderful voice—
as if someone I loved had lifted a window
and called my name.

The streets wash over me like waves.
I sail in the boat of factories and sparrows
out of sight.

A Plea to White Men to Join the March on Washington, August 28, 1963

At nightfall
there is a soft knocking
on the doors—

the great wooden doors,
hammered shut
and sealed
all these years—

And outside
there are shouts, faces,
cities and lonely roads.
Millions of people
are alive
and go from house to house
knocking on the doors.

Outside
men's hopes
hold out their hands to you—
worn hands, with blackness in the folds
of the knuckles;
with great nails, smashed and disfigured
as if hit with a hammer.

Where are you?

The Night

Like old shadows,
highways of diseased moonlight—
like an ancient sore
torn out of the sky,
the night begins to enter us.

And within nerves there is a stirring of strange boots.
Silently, in the blackness, a rifleman
smelling of decay knocks on the door of his room
untouched since World War II.

On a dark stairway, a man stares into abandoned apartments
looking for the praise of his father.
Slowly, the mind opens
and blood vessels reach out
like huge trees, touching the dark.

Alone.
Across the great distance of dreams
men cannot help each other.
And there is that silence—
as if a mute were dragged under by the sea.

Remedy for a Guy Who's Sick of His Line of Work

Beautiful labor, man! That's
what we need.
The dark, lovely work that's done in dreams
where nothing is petty;
as it's done invisibly
in roots of trees.

Forget about necessities.
Walk elsewhere. Hat off.
Ready to be rained on.
Hunched over, jubilant,
as if your legs were translating the lines
of an unknown poet.

Willimantic, Conn.

A company spokesman
has denied
the rumor
that all men are sailors.

He has explained
that the desert is loved
by men
and that employees
are naturally attracted to dust.
He said that clerks
were part of the caravan
of blank eyes.

As for strange dreams
of ships
and impossible fish,
he said they were a direct consequence
of wetting the lips
too often.

Evening

At the bus stop, a man I know
tries to wipe off the heavy dust that
has fallen on him

with this rag of a poem.

Distinguished contemporary poetry in cloth and paperback editions

ALAN ANSEN: *Disorderly Houses* (1961)

JOHN ASHBERY: *The Tennis Court Oath* (1962)

ROBERT BAGG: *Madonna of the Cello* (1961)

ROBERT BLY: *Silence in the Snowy Fields* (1962)

TURNER CASSITY: *Watchboy, What of the Night?* (1966)

TRAM COMBS: *saint thomas. poems.* (1965)

DONALD DAVIE: *Events and Wisdoms* (1965); *New and Selected Poems* (1961)

JAMES DICKEY: *Buckdancer's Choice* (1965) [National Book Award in Poetry, 1966]; *Drowning With Others* (1962); *Helmets* (1964)

DAVID FERRY: *On the Way to the Island* (1960)

ROBERT FRANCIS: *The Orb Weaver* (1960)

JOHN HAINES: *Winter News* (1966)

RICHARD HOWARD: *Quantities* (1962)

BARBARA HOWES: *Light and Dark* (1959)

DAVID IGNATOW: *Figures of the Human* (1964); *Say Pardon* (1961)

DONALD JUSTICE: *Night Light* (1967); *The Summer Anniversaries* (1960) [A Lamont Poetry Selection]

CHESTER KALLMAN: *Absent and Present* (1963)

LOU LIPSITZ: *Cold Water* (1967)

VASSAR MILLER: *My Bones Being Wiser* (1963); *Wage War on Silence* (1960)

W. R. MOSES: *Identities* (1965)

DONALD PETERSEN: *The Spectral Boy* (1964)

HYAM PLUTZIK: *Apples from Shinar* (1959)

VERN RUTSALA: *The Window* (1964)

HARVEY SHAPIRO: *Battle Report* (1966)

JON SILKIN: *Poems New and Selected* (1966)

LOUIS SIMPSON: *At the End of the Open Road* (1963) [Pulitzer Prize in Poetry, 1964]; *A Dream of Governors* (1959)

JAMES WRIGHT: *The Branch Will Not Break* (1963); *Saint Judas* (1959)